Families Around the World

Written by
Margriet Ruurs

Illustrated by
Jessica Rae Gordon

Kids Can Press

For my whole family, especially Nico and Aidan — M.R.

For my wonderful family and for Jesse, who has been so supportive — J.R.G.

Acknowledgments

Thank you to my editor Valerie Wyatt for guiding me through the labyrinth of language. And a very special thank you to the families from around the world who so generously shared their stories with me. Their lives form the basis of my text. Their generosity in sharing a glimpse of their culture made this book possible.

Canada: Jessica Lu
Mexico: Cindy Albaugh, Larka Tetens and the people of Chumpon
Brazil: Cristiana Jurgensen
England: Rachel Hanna
France: Lucie Bridonneau
Poland: Joanna Podwójna
Israel: the Sharon family
Saudi Arabia: Alkawthar Alshams
Kenya: Rosemary Kinyanjui
Pakistan: Syeda Basarat Kazim, Zaib Husain and family
Mongolia: Eggie Bayandorj, Michele Moller and Jambyn Dashdondog
South Korea: Greg Samborksi and family, Choonghee Ryu and family

First paperback edition 2017

Text © 2014 Margriet Ruurs
Illustrations © 2014 Jessica Rae Gordon

Kids Can Press gratefully acknowledges the financial support of the Government of Ontario, through Ontario Creates; the Ontario Arts Council; the Canada Council for the Arts; and the Government of Canada for our publishing activity.

Published in Canada and the U.S. by Kids Can Press Ltd.
25 Dockside Drive, Toronto, ON M5A 0B5

Kids Can Press is a Corus Entertainment Inc. company

www.kidscanpress.com

Edited by Valerie Wyatt
Designed by Marie Bartholomew

Printed and bound in Shenzhen, China, in 12/2019 by C & C Offset

CM 14 09876543
CM PA 17 09876543

Library and Archives Canada Cataloguing in Publication

Ruurs, Margriet, 1952–, author
Families around the world / written by Margriet Ruurs ; illustrated by Jessica Rae Gordon. — First paperback edition 2017.

(Around the world)
ISBN 978-1-894786-57-7 (bound)   ISBN 978-1-77138-807-8 (paperback)

1. Families — Juvenile literature. 2. Children — Social life and customs — Juvenile literature.
I. Rae Gordon, Jessica, 1981–, illustrator II. Title.

HQ744.R88 2017   j306.85   C2016-905175-7

Contents

Families Around the World

What can you do to promote world peace?
Go home and love your family!

— Mother Teresa

Families around the world
are different and yet the same.
Some have one child, a mom and a dad.
Others have only one parent or lots of kids.
And some have two moms or two dads.

You may be born into your family, or you may
be adopted. Your family may be big or small.
Sometimes grandparents, aunts, uncles and
cousins all share a family home.

Families love
and support you.
They help you to
discover the world.

No matter which language you speak,
whether you read the Qur'an or the Bible,
pray to Buddha or God or not at all,
live in a house, a hut or a palace,
you are part of a special family!

Come and meet these children and their families.

Ming Chieh
Canada

Jane
England

Ryan
U.S.A.

Jean-Luc
France

J-Ch'eel
Mexico

Cristiana & Antonio
Brazil

Nkoitoi
Kenya

Sanne
Netherlands

Zofia
Poland

Gilad
Israel

Baatar
Mongolia

Ji Eun
South Korea

Murtaza & Zaib
Pakistan

Zahra
Saudi Arabia

7

Ming Chieh's family came from China to live in Vancouver, Canada.

Hello! *Nǐ hǎo!*

My family came to Vancouver
on an airplane. It was a long flight.

My brother and I had to learn
English fast, to help our parents.
Now we speak Mandarin to relatives in
China but make jokes in English at home
and eat lasagna with chopsticks.

Some of my friends at school were born in Canada.
But others came from far away, too.
We swap snacks at lunchtime —
mooncakes for carrot sticks,
rice balls for chocolate chip cookies.

I love to go hiking with
my family in the mountains.
Once, we even spotted a black bear!

Ryan's family runs a cattle ranch in Texas, U.S.A.

Hi!

Sometimes I ride with Dad
on the tractor to check on our cattle.
We have hundreds of cows and steers —
Texas longhorns.

We also have one sheep.
Lambert is all mine,
even though my sister, Rachel,
helps to feed and brush him.
I will enter him in the fall fair.
I hope he wins a ribbon!

On our farm we grow corn, beets,
potatoes, beans and peas.
I help with weeding
and with eating them, too.

We never go on big trips.
There's too much work on a ranch.
But when my family gathers for dinner,
there's no place in the world I'd rather be.

11

J-Chee's family lives in a Maya village in Mexico.

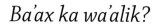

Ba'ax ka wa'alik?

The rooster crows.
I roll out of my hammock.
Papá is still snoring,
but *Mamá* is awake.

I gather eggs while *Mamá*
fries *tortillas* for breakfast.
I put on my *huipil* and help my
little brother Carlos get ready for school.
J-Mulix is too little and stays home.

At home we speak Mayan but at
school we learn in Spanish.
I like history best.
Stories about temples and ruins
make me think of our ancestors
who lived in this very same
spot in the jungle.

After school we walk down the
dusty lane through our village.
I hold Carlos's hand.
Friends and cousins join
us along the way.

Cristiana and Antonio's family lives near Rio de Janeiro, Brazil.

Beleza?

On Sunday *Mãe* makes *farofa*.
Pai cooks meat on the grill.
We take turns stirring the beans in a big pot.
The whole family is coming for dinner!

When our grandparents arrive,
we listen to their stories
while we sip *maracujá* juice.

My aunt wants to kiss us,
but we run to greet our cousins.
We play tag and swing from vines.
We hide under the porch, even though
we are wearing our good Sunday clothes.

When we hear the uncles singing,
we know dinner is ready.
I eat so much my belly aches!
Then we dance, laugh and talk
as the stars come out.

Jane's family lives in a small village in England.

Hello!

On days when Mummy and Daddy work, our auntie looks after us. I play in the park while Emmanuel naps in his pram.

After tea and sandwiches, we ride the bus into the city to my ballet lesson.

When Mummy and Daddy come home
from work, we do a puzzle together,
and Dad builds towers with Emmanuel.
Sometimes I talk on the computer with
my grandmother who lives in Nigeria.
I sing her songs that I learned in school.

At bedtime we have a
bath with bubbles.
Then Mummy reads us Bible
stories until we fall asleep.

Sanne's family lives outside Amsterdam in the Netherlands.

Hoi!

I love weekends. No school!
Sometimes our mothers take
my brother, Joris, and me
on the tram into the city.
We visit a museum
or eat *pannekoeken* on a boat.

Other times we ride our bikes
to the petting zoo, to a playground
or just to another village.

Once, we went inside
a windmill to see how it works.
I loved the creaking and
grinding of the wooden gears.

On Sunday we ride our bikes
to the care home where *Oma* lives.
She doesn't remember my name anymore,
but she gives us cookies from an old tin.
I tell her stories that make her smile.

Jean-Luc's family lives in Paris, France.

Bonjour!

Most of the day I am in school.
My teacher is strict, but I like her.

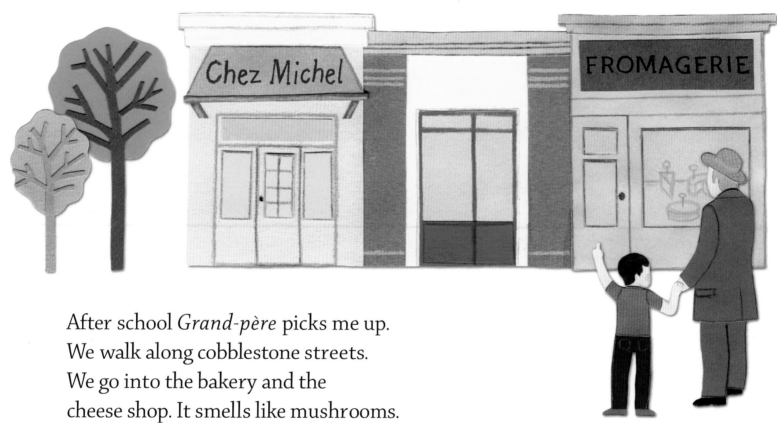

After school *Grand-père* picks me up.
We walk along cobblestone streets.
We go into the bakery and the
cheese shop. It smells like mushrooms.

We buy warm chestnuts to eat in the park.
I play with my friends, and
Grand-père does, too.

Papa arrives at *Grand-père*'s house
as we are making dinner.
We eat around the big wooden table
and talk about our day.
Then *Papa* and I ride
the *Métro* home.

Zofia's family lives in a small town in Poland.

Dzień dobry!

Sunday is my favorite day.
My family walks to church.
The stores are closed.
The town is quiet,
except for church bells ringing out over rooftops.

Back home the house smells good.
Beet soup bubbles on the stove.
I help to cut circles of dough
to make my favorite food — *pierogi*!
Mamusia stuffs them with potatoes and cheese.

Then we all go for a
walk in the woods.
We gather fall leaves
and mushrooms.
My nose turns red from the cold.

In the evening *Tata* listens to classical music.
Mamusia knits a warm sweater.
My brother, Wiktor, and I play video games
until our parents remember it is bedtime!

Gilad's family lives on a *kibbutz* in Israel.

Shalom!

Our *kibbutz* is like a village
where everyone works together.
We have our own house,
but we all eat
in one big dining room.

After school my friends and I walk around
the *kibbutz*, singing songs and laughing.
We eat orange rinds with coconut
and play tag.

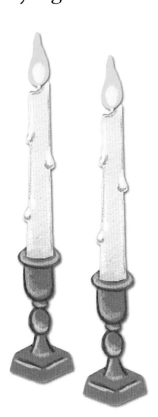

Every Friday night we have *Shabbat*.
We gather just before sunset
to light candles and sing songs.

It makes me feel good
to be part of this big family.

Zahra's family lives in an old city in Saudi Arabia.

Assalamu Alaikum!

Our family wakes before sunrise to pray,
to get ready for a new day.
Ummi kisses us goodbye
and wishes us well at school.
We hurry off — school
starts at 6:30 a.m.

I like computer class and
memorizing verses from the Qur'an.
My favorite thing is to
read stories about other countries.
But I don't like homework!

On Thursday night our weekend
starts with a big family meal.
Then my cousins and I play
hide-and-seek and soccer in the backyard.

At sunset we do our prayers,
as we do five times a day.
When I go to sleep I dream of
traveling the world one day.

Nkoitoi's family lives in a Maasai village in Kenya.

Sopa!

The sun is not up yet, but I am.
The rooster crowed me awake.
I tiptoe outside to fetch water for tea.
Once the sun rises,
I gather firewood,
so we can cook *ugali* for lunch.

I look after our family goat.
Her kids jump for joy and nearly
butt the water jug out of my hands.

Auntie teaches us to read and count
while the mothers weave baskets.

At night I listen to stories the elders tell.
They say that the times are changing,
but I hope some things will stay the same.

Murtaza, Zaib and their family live in Lahore, Pakistan.

Assalamu Alaikum!

Ammi wakes us early every morning to get ready for school.

After school our father picks us up.
Today he has a surprise.
We ride through busy traffic.
Are we going to a soccer match?
To the museum?

No! *Abba* drives us
to the village where he was born.
He shows us where he lived
and went to school.
We see the roses Grandfather planted
when *Abba* was a boy.

Back home we have lots to tell our family.
Then we read from the Qur'an together,
and our parents tuck us into bed.
Tomorrow, *Inshallah*, will bring new adventures.

Baatar is part of a nomadic family in the Gobi Desert of Mongolia.

Sain bain uu!

My family lives in a *ger*, a round tent. On the stove, there is always mutton soup and hot water to make salty tea.